AF317019

STARDOM CHRONICLES

STARDOM CHRONICLES

SERAPHINA WILDE

CONTENTS

1 Introduction 1

2 Chapter 1: The Birth of Icons 3

3 Chapter 2: The Climb to Stardom 7

4 Chapter 3: Peak of Success 11

5 Chapter 4: The Dark Side of Fame 15

6 Chapter 5: Managing the Downfall 19

7 Chapter 6: Legacy and Impact 23

8 Conclusion 27

First Printing, 2024

CHAPTER 1

Introduction

The objective of our book titled 'Stardom Chronicles: The Rise and Fall of Famous Icons' is to present the journey of some of these icons, which we find is required to understand the specialized functioning of the world of stardom. In the very inception of the activities of stars, we need to recognize the waning of their powers and position once they rise high to greet the world around them and steer clear of them. We need to regard the socially produced discernment of the rise and fall of icons as a variety of the administrative clutch of the norms defining the appropriate and the unsuitably considered conditions of the world of stardom. The rise and fall of these stars are as a result of the tabloid information encompassing their arguments or misdemeanors but of the communicative practices of a legion of fictional personalities ceaselessly insinuating the relevance or pointlessness of their activities.

It is intriguing to follow the journey of the rise and fall of famous icons in the ever-growing corpus of creative work. The chronicles of such figures take us on the winding paths of their lives, which are studded with immense riches, fame, and notoriety, as well as the flip side bereft with heartaches, stress, and despair. Their journeys, like those of celestial personalities, invariably affect the happenings in the world of stardom. The ingenuity of their work lays down few golden stepping stones which lead others beyond the horizons of the mundane. Many an icon, in concert with their erstwhile stellar popularity, age and fall in the eyes of the public and eventually choose to lead lives distanced from the reaches of the fierce light gazed upon them.

CHAPTER 2

Chapter 1: The Birth of Icons

Stardom, especially the kind that breeds mega-fame, isn't something that happens in puberty. Icons that become larger than life have their formative years. They have favorite music and movies and people who make them tick. Stardom Chronicles are the early, chronologically arranged histories of big names of our time, names that we've become so used to they look as though they have been engraved in history. But before they became history, they did their round of obscurity, knocking on closed doors and getting rejected because there were no spots for them amongst the chosen. This is where it started; before it's forever frozen in celluloid, Crescograph paper, and Biograph magazine covers.

I'm interested in influence. Early movie stars watch other early movie stars, not movie stars that were yet to come. They really can't because they haven't had time. Yet we have become so used to looking at biographies of our icons as if their future can be foreshadowed in their past. Fame was created in the front rows where the arrivistes were sitting; not in the combat of dreams and rivals. We're not in the future; we're in the present, scraping at the lice of the past. We tell ourselves we're making introductions to the future, but we trip back to the origins of celebrity inasmuch as atavism of the rich and famous is programmed in our very DNA that we had fellowship even when there was none. Icons are not born, they're made. And nobody, certainly not actors, gets any further than the city limits without roadmaps. This is their roadmap. The breadcrumb. The journey. I'm interested in influence. The long and winding road that brought the likes of Halle Berry and Johnny Depp and others whose stories we think we know down. First they had to arrive.

Early Influences

Numerous factors can shape an individual's emergence as a famous icon. Although seemingly unable to pinpoint any major influencers, many famous figures compensate for such absences by invoking themselves or by identifying impersonal forces such as injustices, economic trends, spirituality, and other similar impersonal forces.

Common are the narratives of famous figures who invoked what seemed like magnum force entities such as genetics, destiny, and other reformist or failure narratives. Influences mentioned by famous figures varied. Madam C.J. Walker, for example, credited herself as the sole architect responsible for her ascent to the wealthy elite. She used plots to remove cruelty and bitterness. Jackie Robinson also wrote a serialized autobiography but would regularly invoke divine powers. "I am not saying that I was chosen by God alone to accomplish this sensational task," Rocky Kubat observed, "but one had to be selected. God chose me to jump from obscurity and poverty to riches and celebrity, and I was fully prepared to accept His mandate." The famous magician Harvey Leroy "The Great" Keller insisted that "I was destined to be a star, to make it to the top. A poor boy from Monrovia was the dream of Hollywood, this great star," he explained. In some versions of his unlikely encounter, magic and supernatural influences play a powerful role in the shaping of the minds, talents, and appearances of famous figures.

Initial Breakthroughs

Since the 1980s in Japan, a host of so-called idols with pretty, cool, and charismatic personalities that get popular amongst young boys and girls have emerged. Idols whose names are known all across Japan have been given the distinction of "big idols," and have come to embody Japan's idol industry. Many big idols have appeared and taken the showbiz industry by storm over the years. However, all showbiz industry big idols need to make an initial breakthrough at the start of their careers that strikes a chord with the masses, and there is a fascinating tale behind each one.

Although the idol industry was destroyed by the end of the "Heisei period," the big idols who shaped the time also have their own peculiar histories. They were at the forefront of entertainment during the bubble period of the late 1980s. Some have transcended mere lucrativeness and have lived lives that are somewhat separate from others. If there is a singular reason they became so famous, it would most likely be because they specialized in singing. Singing, unlike the world of acting, is easier for one to show their depth and range as an artist while responding to emotional stimuli. When they moved people, it was through the power of their singing that managed to ignite a passionate audience-seeking era throughout the 1980s in Japan. The testament to their significance remains the fact that the world where the likes of Moritaka Chisato, Sawada Kenji, Kuroyama Shimotsukin, and others played, although it was changed in its nature, has remained a multi-billion yen commercial field to this date.

CHAPTER 3

Chapter 2: The Climb to Stardom

Even in the case of tabloid superstars, every one of today's icons spent years carefully selecting and building their brands. As they ascended into stardom, members of the film, music, and celebrity industries encountered professionals who polished their images, advised their career choices, drafted their contracts, and developed diversification protocols in case of cancellation. In sum, stars have been strategically sculpted, often from childhood. It thus makes sense to track the strategic brand-building process which has directed Galliano, Gervais, GaGa, and indeed, many others from the straight channels of fame into the sturdier canals of iconic stardom.

By the time an icon reaches the stardom arena, they have, through necessity, interfaced with the mechanisms and operatives of the media careers system. Certainly, we can point to moments when certain public figures become suddenly exoticized: Julian Clary entered the British 'showbiz' pages as the 'comic in cowboy gear; Morrissey, in praise of the virtues of celibacy, graced the cover of Smash Hits'... but across a media career, these moments are rare. Most often, stars rise more gradually into their stardom. People who could be iconic stars are recruited into institutional training programs or become corporate interns. The people they meet are trusted as mentors and friends; over the years, they move across the media industries, making contacts and developing a fan base in different locations.

Building a Brand

As has been suggested before, no one gets to be a star accidentally. Actors, musicians, and other entertainers, as well as professional athletes, invest time and effort to manage their image and convey that image to the public. The same is true of other "celebrities," including business leaders and international criminals. These efforts are part of an attempt to construct a so-called personal brand and to convince and assure others that they really are as advertised.

Ignoring individuals who are born into families already famous, iconic, or established as a brand (such as the Kardashian-Jenners), almost everyone else has to work themselves to the bone just to be recognized as larger-than-life, let alone to be regarded as god-like in their glory. Very few ordinary mortals can even think about the status of those held in iconic regard by others. That is, brand image only accrues and accumulates over time but also with the right kind of promotional and public relations activities and available viral multimedial platforms. For their part to become new, icons develop, advance, enhance, promote, and consummate their individual persona into a highly marked "brand." Their "celebritisation" or "iconisation" becomes "manipulation" in the sense of taking hold of the reins to gain control of the promotional development of a unique "identity" befitting the chewed, up-chucked, and eaten hypercompetitive, "bifurcative" scenography of the spectacular capitalist, liberal-political, democratic, marketised society. The icon brand acts as a rod protecting the star from the rusty decay of the historic, primary star persona. The latter can shrivel up into nothing, unless pumped up on a constant rich diet of valuable talent and ingenuity to keep it gleaming, vital, energetic and wanted.

Media Exposure

Media publicity plays a crucial role in the making of an icon because of the dominance of the visual. Footage of Elvis appeared on television in the fifties, and because television is a mass medium, this meant that Elvis became known to billions. In the same way, the Beatles' success also rode the tiny wave of fashionability only this time it was the conquest of America, as Beatle iconology. The obvious aspect in links with this is the introduction of new filmic formats of filming during the sixties as in 'populuxe', such as in fulsome Technicolor. The old and venerable black-and-white glamour of yesteryear had kept movie stars special and cloaked in mystery. One key element of this new film footage was that it was usually of some press conference, which in itself was an older and populist medium with cameras everywhere even before the days of TV came to pass. Furthermore, the fact of showing press conferences in full colour also has the advantage of concentrating on facial defects or facial beauty in a way that black-and-white concealment does not and never did. The adopting of television media has been mainly conducted by the music and film industries. The long complications of ritual and amortization has always dictated traditional investment in mass media - broadly with diminishing explosive returns for the effort. But the many stars who have risen from TV talent programs can be seen as an example of how media exposure can further expand the limelight. Therefore, in order for a singer to become an icon, they should pass through the medium. Those icons who have channeled their career through media exposure from Britain include the Beatles, Elton John, David Bowie, and Boy George. As mentioned above, the problem with the current media exposure is that due to the prescriptive nature of the media, a manifestation as whimsical and spontaneous would only excite the audience in as far as a reputable and pragmatic marketing approach negotiates a subcultural honor for the icon as an outline negotiation on terms.

CHAPTER 4

Chapter 3: Peak of Success

In Chapter 3, the paper will recap the peak of fame for the identified icons. It will summarize how they were currently the most famous and successful in their fields, their style, and significant or iconic achievements they made during this period.

I: The Golden Ages

King of Pop: Michael Jackson was the world's most successful music artist during the early 1980s at the height of the disco craze and during the early 90s explosion of new jack swing. Several critics have cited him as the "King of Pop" due to his worldwide impact on the music industry history and the rise of pop music in the 1980s and 1990s. Even today Michael and especially his album 'Thriller' is still known and celebrated globally.

II: Brief Overview: Epoch of Success

Emancipated Woman: Dita Von Teese currently propagates 'a positive message about female sexuality', portraying herself as a glamorous seductress, always found draped in haute couture outfits. Von Teese's iconic style definitely has had a huge impact, as she is seen as a leading figure in reviving the burlesque scene from obscurity. As a result, women have begun to visit the salon again.

Surrealist Mastermind: H. R. Giger is deemed 'visionary, gifted and versatile' by critics. His paintings and sculptures have inspired more than one generation, and he is a regular figure at numerous concerts promoting his art. In addition, he has received a consistent amount of public collaboration ranging from album covers to films in Hollywood. Furthermore, many virtual reality games, starting off with the Alien franchise, have journeyed to Gigerland. Bears proudly carrying the Giger legacy are H. R. Giger's La Abeja (painter), Alejandro Lübrio (painter), Carmen Isasi (textile artist), Stefanie Herr (painter), Alice Gironi and Anesj Antoniv-Oudak.

Iconic Achievements

One of the things we should always be proud of is the remarkable achievements and milestones reached by our illustrious stars, as they all have done a lot and must be earned. Previous studies have compiled or examined some major accomplishments achieved by reputable personalities in various domains. For example, focused on examining articles that synthesised previous sports Big Data studies and investigated football iconicity by examining sports personalities' unique achievements contained in their Wikipedia profiles across different domains. By way of illustration, as of July 2019, Lionel Messi, an Argentine Footballer for both Paris Saint-Germain and the Argentine National Team, holds the record in the following categories: a record 7 Ballon D'Or, a record 5 Golden Shoes, most La Liga titles, most Pichichi Trophy won, most La Liga Assists, and most European Golden Shoes in a single season, Major Championships Won, Most Hat-Tricks in All Competitions, Most Free-Kick Goals,Time Neymar Jr. was an international journalist for Brazil and Lebanon. In comparison, Roger Federer, a Swiss sportsperson, is an international tennis player, and has conquered 20 grand slams and appeared in 31 grand slam finals.

Both authors analyse a substantial amount of textual information, scraping data that spanned 1704 episodes collected over a 12-year period (2007-2018) and 3260 current and former dignitaries from around the world located in a renown-free online encyclopedia that crowdsources its artefacts or knowledge. In light of the spectacle's growing size with entries or articles strewn across sport, film and music, our investigation aims to offer fresh insight into the nature of stars and how they accomplish lasting reputation, with the help of cross-fertilizing various datasets or pieces of information, creativity, computer techniques and techniques, in this day and age and helps organizations extract knowledge-filled data or Big Data and immaturely open chrome doodles and flip the ballificial can be produced.

Global Impact

Stardom Chronicles: The rise and fall of famous icons...and then you could argue for part II of this event (and so forth). Global Impact is confirmed. I didn't particularly set out on a major educational drive with or directed at the case study of Goldies Arts Award, although I did have a Classics Review of relevant topics up my sleeve for a while now, and I have also been sharing Arts Award Activity Logs and the National Qualification with community partners involved in Disability Arts and products like She Rocola. It was in fact a case of FaB pulling back to reveal its workings – who's who, what are the stories, how is it done; and the breadth of artists provided added gravitas, even if most were "linear" like me and not "full spirally whirly whorled" like prolific teadrinker.

I also have many years experience of industry for interests sakes. It is but a small step for woman, but I would have avoided it completely if I had been able! It seems important to offer participants incentives at least of some kind because there needs to be some motivation for participation in any diary study, and it may also be important as an Arts Award project too. Goldies happened to be touring their veterans (who remember the 1940s) throughout the South West and we learned about the elderly which was horrific. They were confessional and we collected many stories, wanting the government to fund the living history of the very old before it is lost. We have good contacts with Wiltshire College on this. We interviewed Cie Exarteko in person with no compression.

CHAPTER 5

Chapter 4: The Dark Side of Fame

In this age of influencers and fandom, it is easy to forget the path recent and living icons have had to travel. Although a world of privilege and luxury might be seen now, stirred scandals, and a quest for eternal beauty or youth are part of the journey many stick diligently to erase from public memory. The ambition of Stardom Chronicles is to indirectly tail an array of bittersweet and bitter-smelling stories: growing suicide rates as a result of mental breakdowns; sexual harassment and abuse; Botox accidents; destructive trends; physical attacks; misuse of assets and underbelly debts. A depth of insight apart, the intention is not to harm or try celebrities in absentia. The chapter aims to bring across the multifaceted drawbacks the access to a duteous career involves. The pain behind the facade is a given we are often unconsciously participating in.

This inclusion turns its focus from the pitch of singing voices to the dark side of stardom: the unsustainability of managing the onslaught of scandals, the fame attached to the name of the fair-skinned stars. So-called anti-trainers, the facial care business for at least one decade, has seen a decrease in the number of books despite being ill with Botox, saturated fillers or laser techniques. The success rate of this market made a hostile acquisition by a few global pharmaceuticals an easier process in a market that relies on contestation and what is considered as black ops-unit revenues. The transformation to a "choice market" at the express wish of those who are commercially accounted for also means that lack of knowledge can result in the acquisition of permanent changes, dangerous products, and death.

Scandals and Controversies

Over time, a few events regarding famous Theseus have shaped a history or public opinion about them, here are some examples. Behaviour. Maria Callas was one of the world's greatest sopranos who began her Opera singing career in Athens at the age of 17. In 1950 she made her debut in Italy and, just two years later, sung at the San Francisco Opera. infuriated by her lack of recognition, she returned to perform in the land of her birth: the United States. The Metropolitan Opera, where Maria Callas appeared, attracted attention by broadcasting performances of her live on television. Her powerful voice and her presence made her internationally famous. Little by little though, Callas's health began to deteriorate, a factor which ultimately led to the downfall of her career. She died age 53 in Paris. The controversial Mistaken Identitythought to be likely due to Maria Callas's affair with another woman's husband, eventually drove her from the United States on October 2,1970

Involvement in a scandal. Charlie Chaplin first arrived in American in 1910 and he returned time and again until purchasing a Hollywood house in 1919. In 1942 Chaplin became embroiled in a scandalous legal case involving his relationship with a young actress named Joan Berry and spent over seven months in court. The Jury of six men and six women ruled in his favor, finding he did not encourage Joan Berry to be a prostitute or the arrange for her to have an abortion. Until his death Chaplin was followed continuously by the FBI, and the case records were sealed for fifty years, order by the federal justice system. In addition to King Solomon and Queen of Sheba, the annual reports of the Mid-Victorian Society in England, charlie chaplain had a Battle of Forces, are the warrior of peace left out, Controversial Affairs. It was rumored that Mata Hari engaged in espionage during world war1, while serving as a dutch courtesan in Paris, Mata Hari was involved in three affairs with high-ranking military officers from three different countries, a fact which increased the social scandal. She also supported herself during world war 1 by working as a courtesan to both French and German officers. Her relationships with powerful men frequently opened the doors to diplomatic and military information that she might not have otherwise obtained. However, the day before her fifty-eighth birthday she was taken before a firing squad and executed, for being a German spy.

Mental Health Challenges

As someone involved in the arts or entertainment industry, it is not uncommon to have to juggle between grueling routines, unsociable hours, and demanding schedules. Mental health issues are widespread in the fast-paced entertainment world, and evidence shows that mental illness issues have and continue to increase. The lifestyle of entertainment can bring plenty of money and other means of personal development. But as any entertainment industry worker knows, one's mental wellbeing enters a different world.

More often than not, the approach to writing about famous icons is of a personal nature; the effect of their music, dancing, or acting on their particular writer; however, little focus is placed on their battles with their own fame, or at least how it mentally affects the stars. In recent years, focus has turned to these issues. But it is often not the prospect of a mental issue that drives a performer to take their own life, it is the creativity and hard work that it takes to reach such an emotional low that make one feel beyond help. Actress and activist Carrie Fisher is a prime example of somebody who is widely recognized to have struggled with mental health due to the pressure of her stardom. The cause of such emotional states is perpetuated not only by the artists themselves and those close to them, but by the media attention which surrounds the situation. Author Philip Hoare pointed out that in sections of the media, artists look ever nearer to the grave; "The time has come for us to face into the fact that those whom we worship in life we also regale in death, with fewer facts and even more barren speculation. Sameness has sated us of logic." Public profile – especially its speculative inquiries into health or sanity – can prove to be a whole new role of fame. For Fisher, who at the current date refuses to give up acting despite quitting four times, the media's actions are irritating, not a personal issue. For most others, the attention is overwhelming – especially as the interest and speculation is often inaccurate as well as constant.

CHAPTER 6

Chapter 5: Managing the Downfall

Once the negative information has been exposed, it cannot be untold. So, rather than trying to manage it through eradication, the affected icon has to comply and make the best of it. Goffman discusses how it is possible to accept a change in status and make the most of the new situation if the individual with the affected reputation adapts their presentation of self to fit in with that change in status. As well as developing an appropriate performance of the self, the individual may also strive to change the expressive equipment that he or she uses to present themselves to the world.

In chapter two, we considered how an individual trains and refines themselves to give a performance that is considered to be a reflection of their 'true' self. However, through coaching, therapy, or surgery, such an individual may be able to change that presentation of self as part of internalizing that change in status. Therefore, in order to understand how individuals try to manage the effect that they may have if they have incomplete ability to make a genuine performance, we looked at processes of identity transformation in chapter three. Goffman's plight to do this differently is not available to all.

We drew on theory which focuses on the specializes indispensability self to confirmation of society.

Habitual issues of difference depend not only upon identity and performance; they also create oppositions of space eruptions confile of spatial political and ethnical identities. The sometimes associations with particular postulated in aside chapter five, as a form of severity, a sentence that affects. The inverse of the deprivation is moderation space; they received the standard performed passage prison for them—status as deportees.

Public Image Rehabilitation

Restoration of their public images is an important concern for most Indian icons. Many of them have faced personal and professional meltdowns in their careers, so public image restoration plays a substantial role in their lives. It is evident that in mainstream society, the main mechanism of image restoration is offering public apologies. These apologies are cited in their behavioral image restoration strategies, as they talk about their attitudes, promises, and responsibilities. They focus on their actions and motivate people to avoid destructive actions and harmful effects. By using functional communication and inducing people's motivations to make amends, they also encourage the public to give them opportunities to expedite and re-establish a good reputation.

Misbehavior conducted by public idols has often resulted in various criticism and negative consequences for themselves and others. An important argument in crisis management is consequently publicity, with research focused on how celebrities are affected when dealing with identification agents and have a substantial part in idiosyncratic stigma and/or conflict for their companies and/or sponsors. Establishment, dilemma resolution, and stakeholders are used by well-known symbols to protect themselves from misconduct.

In current trials outsourced through an organizational and economic awareness prism, this article analyzes methods utilized by well-known stars to refurbish their identification when misconduct is alleged. Celebrity reports were found to aid or alienate the personal, market, and supporters of the news. Mistakes have a lot of time for identifying the outworking transformer and focusing your prospects to be collaborative or canceling, allowing the superstar to triumph over their mistakes.

Career Transition

Aging and the routine nature of fame prescription in a domain are two reasons for the career transition of a popular star. Perhaps a more important aspect is the sheer explosion in avenues of stardom, which makes it possible to continually renew a public identity through the accumulation of different fields. In the past, some ways of stardom were almost wholly distinct, but currently it appears quite possible for someone to be famous in several fields at once, and for several such fields to bear some relation to one another. Hollywood actors have always taken the step into music on occasion, and country music stars have occasionally tried their hand at acting.

But even Michael Jordan seems to offer an example of a particular type of trans-stardom. While the 1955 Grace Kelly starred in several films with Alfred Hitchcock, Jordan lays out the autobiography "For the Love of the Game," published by Simon and Schuster – the same company that published Jim Boeheim's and Foreman's books – in 1998. All around him, superstar athletes are making a foray into film: Will the boundary of fame extend into a new field? Bregman, Cody. 2 5.2.2 Some Examples The sports figures in my narrative would be examples of one type of career transition, branching out into other fields during or after athletic stardom. A non-athlete, albeit a prima donna, Bessie Smith performed and recorded songs written by any number of individuals, including WC Handy, Euday Bowman, and another recording artist of the period, Irving "King of Jazz" Kaufman; in addition, she was a regular performer at New York's Hot Cha club, which was frequented by "Fame Attractions" like Lee and J.J. Shubert; see Dettmar 1916: 54; 1917b: 29.

CHAPTER 7

Chapter 6: Legacy and Impact

Famous icons who are remembered in Stardom Chronicles: The Rise and Fall of Famous Icons are fondly remembered by the millions of people who felt forever altered by the legacy of these icons' contributions. With the lasting legacies that have become their lives, these icons have left lasting impacts on the individuals who have also been influenced by the world around them. As producers of the text of Stardom Chronicles: The Rise and Fall of Famous Icons are fans of our own, it is only fitting that for the last section of this book, a real tribute to the fallen will be made. Tears will fall. This chapter reflects on the impacts made by the individuals within in an effort to further underscore the profound nature of our fallen friends of old.

To explore the impacts of our lost loves of old, we must turn to the legacies that have been left by Jack, Marilyn, the Phantom of the Opera, Mervyn, and Humphrey. These individuals have not only played their part in changing culture itself, but probably just as much have inspired the millions of people in multiple countries who've seen their stars to go out and initiate small pieces of their own cultural movements. These impacts may not always have been massive, but the important thing is that the lives of these folks have inspired generations of people to go out and try to do something totally different with their own lives as well.

Enduring Influence

Stardom is much contested; however, one cannot take away what these iconic figures have contributed to popular culture and our social life. The actors, pop stars, and DJs that we have looked at in this work set the wheels of consumption in motion into the twenty-first century. Although the Elvis franchise was the first and is considered one of the best, they were all profitably identified with the marketing machine. The synergy of popular music, film, and branded products is now as much a part of our media landscape as it has ever been.

Today, the sensibility, sociology, and management of celebrity is an important area of academic study. Marketing and PR companies have sprung up to help produce celebrity from the most unlikely material. The emergent mass-mediated culture of the operas in 1780s Britain, the Victorian music hall in the late eighteenth century, silent movies ruled in the 1920s, and popular music from the 1950s coincided and were always-ending modes of vacation and fun. Modern celebrity is, however, a peculiarly doubled yet singular form of holiday, for celebrities engage in hard work and personal sacrifice both to entertain and to give vacation pleasure. And vacationers partially identify with their celebrities, continually moving in and out of the aegis of their flexible identities. These in part constructed icons provide conduits through which we may perform our freedom from solid identity and take our vacations from selfhood. All celebrities endure, having done their work. All icons end.

Cultural Significance

In the popular imagination, icons are often perceived as individuals who fronted bands, who looked and dressed distinctively, and also sang certain songs which are deemed to be iconic. The analysis of their contributions to rock music has always been complex since what one examines is not just a musician (bass player, guitar player, vocalist, or drummer) but also a member of a larger group that fronts a wider musical, artistic, and cultural phenomenon. While some authors were biographers and hence placed more emphasis on the cultural significance of icons, most of the literature on British acid/psychedelic music focused on the historical analysis of a particular acid band, a particular album or track; the influence of American music on the British scene; or on the 'conflict' between American influence and the search for the construction of a British cultural and musical identity. This study would like to reflect on the cultural significance of these icons and on the reasons why they continue to be present and to be considered an influence today.

Still, while acknowledging that these popular musicians have survived as an icon to a 'different' generation represented by the 1990s Britpoppers and by some dance bands, one aspect of them has been overlooked in academic or historical works. To the best of our knowledge, no economic analyses have been developed to date concerning the impact of the resurgence in interest in these individuals and the effect of their bands, albums, and concerts on the wider musical, artistic, and cultural landscape. It is our belief that such an impact does exist, and it is such, but also the magnitude of this impact that we aim to measure in our work. If the acceptance is widespread concerning the statement that an economic impact is present, what remains to be ascertained is its extent. The answer given in our paper, though tentative, is in terms of significant numbers.

CHAPTER 8

Conclusion

From exploring the dark secrets behind blacklisting and drug addiction to questioning why the Hollywood machine crafted some stars as icons, the books in this collection have further explored the 'rise' of the famous icon. History tells us about Marlon Brando revolutionizing acting methods or Elizabeth Taylor's many data posts in tabloid magazines, gossip columns, and Hollywood rags. Icons are the extreme examples of these mega-stars. We mostly hear of these stars that are still iconic, long after they've died. We know them for their acclaim, and even more now for their mistakes. These books offered depth into the lives of stars in all the shoreline of tradition; again fortifying what we already know about them. Norma Jean became Marilyn; Judy married Mickey, then people; Howard Hughes became 'Mr. America'. The stories, rather their arc trajectories, as already delineated in these books, make us question them - not as 'real people', but for the fictions that they are. Judy and Elizabeth are icons because - from a very early age - they have been trained to be synonymous with themselves, and make us ask, then what does that entail?

If the first section 'rising' of famous icons was about blasting the stars into orbit, however they were constructed, now we are concerned with where they will land when the loss of gravity reaches them. The conclusion of this collection of books is 'falling': physically into drug and alcohol grinds, and mentally into larger questions of what celebrity means, and what it has meant to have 'fallen' as a public, un-public, 'nobody'. This collection of books successfully burrowed deeper into the lore and legend of stardom, into the act itself, and its surrounding space. Should we ask 'what is in the canon?', we will know also then, to ask, what is not?

www.ingramcontent.com/pod-product-compliance
Lightning Source LLC
Chambersburg PA
CBHW020753150726
48196CB00023B/757
9798348193591